Homework Ma

Ending Con

Abracadabra! You can add a light ... your child's learning time! *Homework Magic* will help you reinforce important basic phonics skills that will build the foundation for future learning. The one-on-one time you spend teaching your child is an irreplaceable gift that will give him or her the extra knowledge that will lead to self-confident, successful school years.

HOW TO USE THIS BOOK

- Choose a place to work with your child that is comfortable, cozy, and relatively free of distraction. This is special time!
- Remove the "magic wand" from the binding of the book. Tear the perforated lines to create the wand. Set the wand aside until it is time for your child to check his or her answers.
- Make sure your child understands the directions before beginning an activity.
- Invite your child to complete the problems on an activity page in pencil, offering as much help and encouragement as your child needs to feel successful.
- When it is time for your child to check his or her answers, show him or her how to use the wand to reveal the hidden answer. Have fun during this part of your learning time! When your child reveals the correct answer, say *abracadabra!* or *presto!* or *wow!* If your child reveals an answer that differs from his or hers... *Hocus pocus!* Just erase the incorrect answer and rework the problem with your child.

FS111113 Homework Magic—Ending Consonants

23740 Hawthorne Blvd., Torrance, CA 90505

ISBN #0-76820-427-5

Edited by Cindy Barden
Illustrated by Becky J. Radtke
Cover Design by Good Neighbor Press, Inc.

Where's the "b"?

Ending Consonant b

Say the name of each picture. Draw a line from the fishing pole to each picture that ends with the sound of b.

What can a goldfish do that a whale can't?

The "b" Is at the End

Ending Consonant b

Print the answers to the riddles on the lines. Use the words in the word box.

cab bib sub crib cub tub

Babies wear me. What am I?

You take a bath in me. What am I?

I can take you for a ride under the water. What am I?

Babies sleep in me. What am I?

I can take you for a ride on land. What am I?

I am a baby bear. What am I?

What kind of whales live in the Arctic Ocean?

Let's End with a "d"!

Ending Consonant d

Circle the words that end with the letter d. Draw pictures of the words that end in d.

door	Dan
wood	dad
bird	side
made	squid
bread	seed
bride	dice

Why do squids hum when they hear music?

Silly Sea Serpent

Ending Consonant d

Find the words ending in d in the silly sea serpent. Print them on the lines.

What do silly sea serpents eat for lunch?

Dad's Mad!

Ending Consonant d

Look at the picture. Print the correct word in each sentence.

This is my ____________________ .

(sad, dad)

He is ____________________ .

(mad, pad)

My dog was ____________________ .

(bad, lad)

Now my dog is ____________________ .

(sad, had)

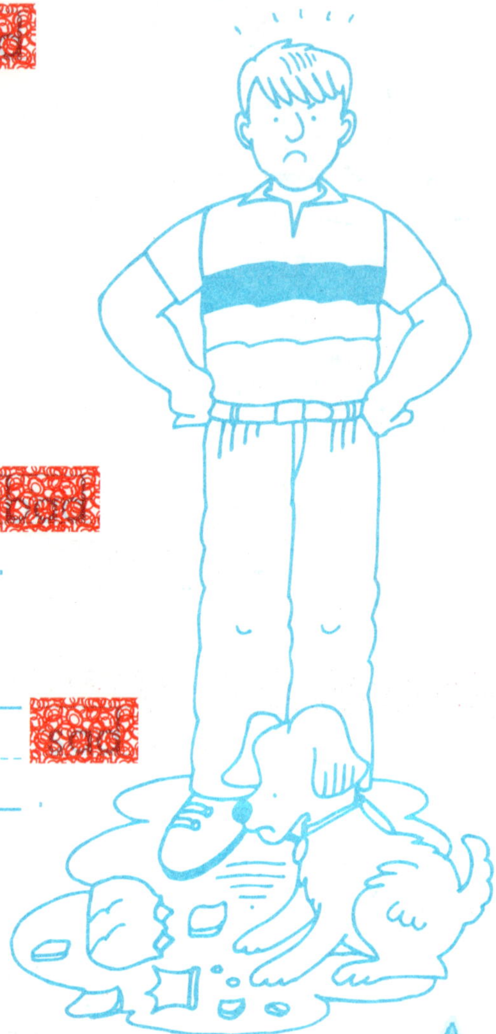

What always follows a shark, day and night, winter and summer?

Fishing for Ending Consonants

Ending Consonants b and d

Finish the word in each boat. Draw a line from the fishing pole to the fish with the correct letter.

What is the brightest fish?

A Fat Fish

Ending Consonant f

Circle the words that end with the letter f. Draw pictures of the words that end in f.

golf		shelf	
fold		after	
fun		scarf	
surf		first	
loaf		leaf	
fast		lift	

What did the whale do after he ate a 300 pound meal?

These End with "f"

Ending Consonant f

Print the answers to the riddles on the lines. Find the words in the starfish.

I grow on a tree.

I am a ________________.

I am a baby cow.

I am called a ________________.

I am like a wild dog.

I am a ________________.

I am one of two equal pieces.

I am a ________________.

Bakers bake me. People eat me.

I am a ________________ of bread.

What kind of fish lives in the sky?

Dogs, Frogs, and Pollywogs!

Ending Consonant g

Say the name of each picture. Print the letter sound you hear at the end of each word. Color the pictures.

g

g

g

g

g

g

What happens to illegally parked frogs?

You're a Good Egg!

Ending Consonant g

Unscramble the letters. Write words ending with g on the lines.

p g i

g g e

t g a

r i g n

i b g

g k i n

Why is a turtle such a strong animal?

Peg, the Digging Pig

Ending Consonant g

Look at the picture. Print the correct word in each sentence.

I am a ______________________.

(jig, pig)

I have on a ______________________.

(wig, fig)

I am going to ______________________.

(dig, fig)

What do you get when you cross a porcupine with a turtle?

Jog, Dog, Jog!

Ending Consonant g

Look at the picture. Print the correct word in each section.

I see a ________________ .

(hog, dog)

He can ________________ .

(log, jog)

See the green ________________ .

(hog, frog)

It is on the ________________ .

(log, jog)

What should you do if 37 frogs are on the back window of your car?

Knock! Knock!

Ending Consonant k

Say the name of each picture. Print the letter sound you hear at the end of each word. Color the pictures.

Which side of a duck has the most feathers?

You "Quack" Me Up!

Ending Consonant k

Say the name of each picture. Does the word end with the sound of the letter k? Circle yes or no.

yes

no

yes

no

yes

no

yes

no

yes

no

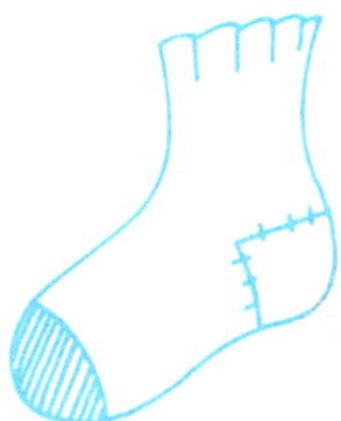

yes

no

Why did the duck go to college?

You're a Doll!

Ending Consonant l

Say the name of each picture. Print the letter sound you hear at the end of each word. Color the pictures.

What fish is worth the most?

Let's Sail to the Mall!

Ending Consonant l

Print the correct word in each sentence. Find the words in the Word Box.

Word Box
mall fall seal

You visit me to shop.

I am a __________.

I can do tricks with a ball.

I am a __________.

I come before winter.

I am __________.

How does a fish become a good piano player?

Small and Tall

Ending Consonants I

Look at the picture. Print the correct word in each sentence.

He is ______________.

(fall, tall)

He has a ______________.

(ball, call)

She is ______________.

(small, wall)

She is on the ______________.

(hall, wall)

What do you call a fish with two knees?

Clam Up!

Ending Consonant m

Print the answers to the riddles on the lines. Find the words in the clam.

I am a cow.

I live on a ______________.

I can help you clean house.

I am a ______________.

You can beat me to music.

I am a ______________.

I marry the bride.

I am the ______________.

What time is it when a whale sits on your bed?

Ham and Eggs

Ending Consonant m

Unscramble the letters. Write words ending with m on the lines.

h m a ____________________

m a j ____________________

o w r m ____________________

r m o o ____________________

d m u r ____________________

m f a r ____________________

What kind of fish can you find in a bird cage?

A Loud Drum

Ending Consonants d and m

Circle the letter you hear at the end of each word.

m
d
r

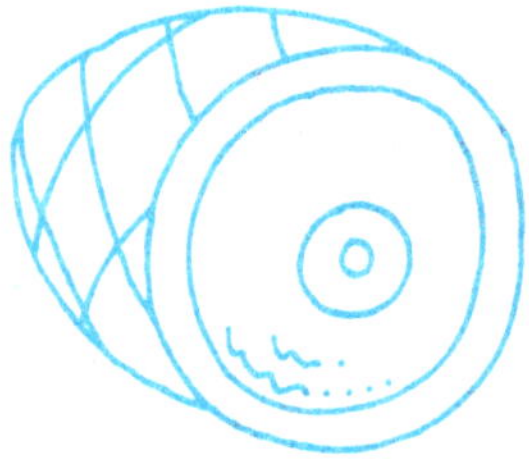

b
d
m

m
d
r

b
d
m

m
d
r

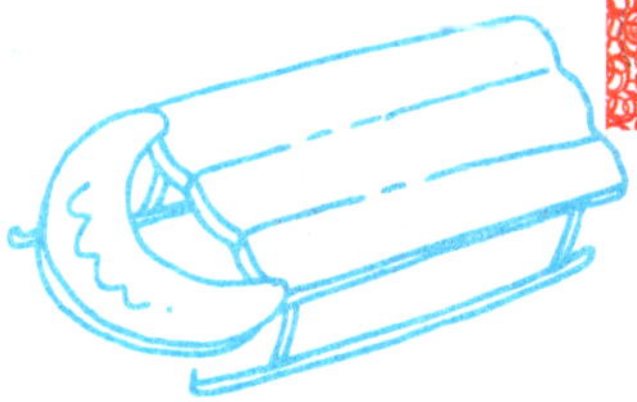

b
d
m

What did one ocean say to the other ocean?

Silly Sea Serpent

Ending Consonant n

Find the words ending in n in the silly sea serpent. Print them on the lines.

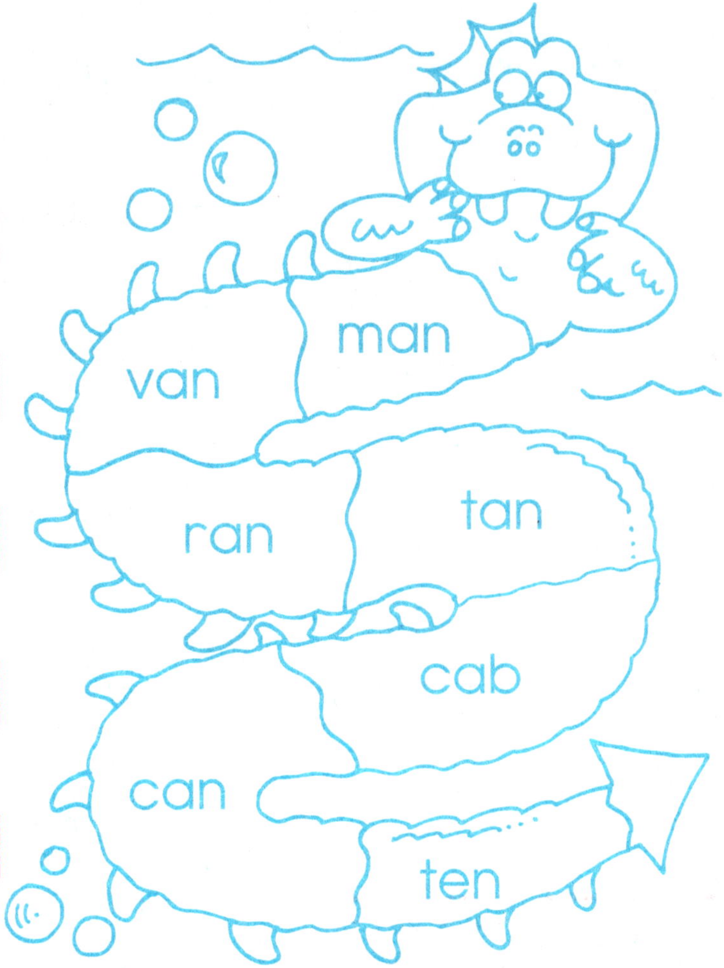

What should you do when a silly sea serpent sneezes?

She's a Fun Clown!

Ending Consonant n

Look at the picture. Print the correct word in each sentence.

This ________________

(clown, down)

________________ has on a ________________ .

(town, gown)

It is ________________ .

(brown, drown)

Will she go to ________________ ?

(town, brown)

Three men fell in the ocean. Only two got their hair wet. Why?

Toot Your Horn and Grin!

Ending Consonant n

Print the answers to the riddles on the lines. Find the words in the umbrella.

I grow on a cob.

____

I am ____________________ .

I am a number.

____

I am ____________________ .

You can spend me.

____

I am a ____________________ .

Push me and I honk.

____

I am a ____________________ .

I am a big smile.

____

I am a ____________________ .

What kind of rocks are at the bottom of the ocean?

A Fine Flag

Ending Consonants g and n

Circle the letter you hear at the end of each word.

n
g
x

n
g
x

n
g
x

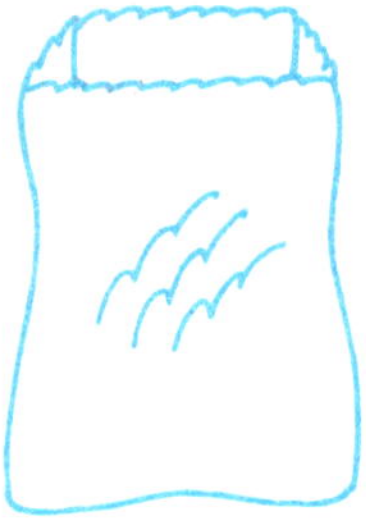

n
g
x

n
g
x

n
g
x

What kind of frog is the meanest?

Hippety Hop!

Ending Consonant p

Say the name of each picture. Print the letter sound you hear at the end of each word.

What kind of bill never needs to be paid?

Ship Shape!

Ending Consonant p

Print the answers to the riddles on the lines. Find the words in the ship.

You can walk up and down on me. ______________

I am a ______________ .

You can do this on one leg.

____

You can ______________ .

You can sail in me.

____

I am a ______________ .

I am a small dog.

____

I am a ______________ .

Where does a seasick ship go?

Meek as a Sheep

Ending Consonants k and p

Say the name of each picture. Print the letter sound you hear at the end of each word.

Why didn't the sailors play cards on the ship?

Let's Review

Ending Consonants l, n, and p

Say the name of each picture. Circle the letter you hear at the end of each word.

p
l
n

p
l
n

p
l
n

p
l
n

p
l
n

p
l
n

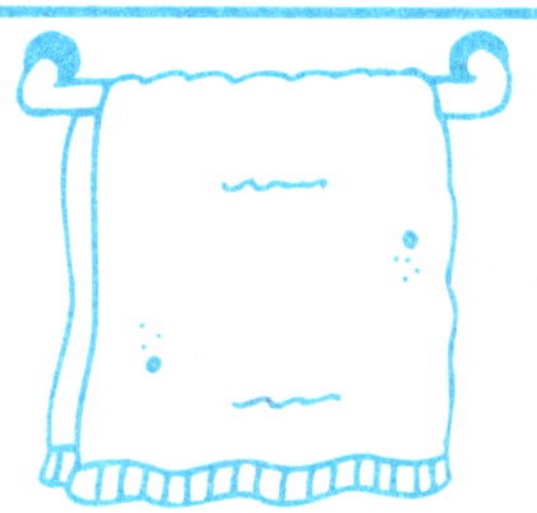

What gets wetter the more it dries?

You're a Phonics Superstar!

Ending Consonant r

Say the name of each picture. Print the letter sound you hear at the end of each word. Color the pictures.

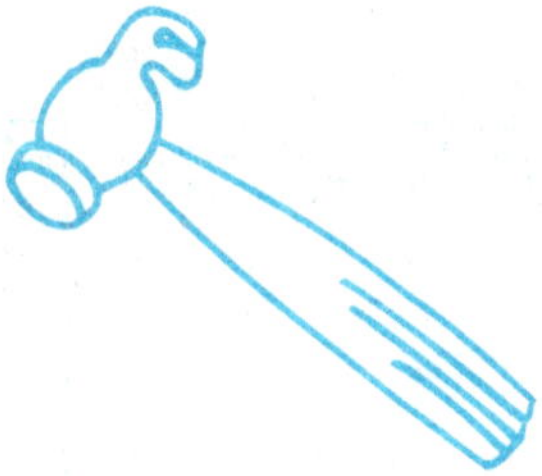

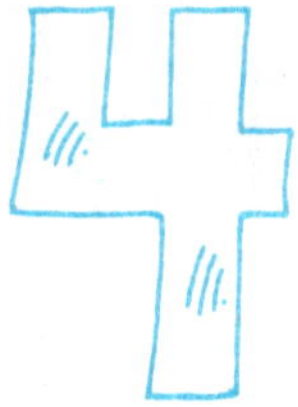

How can you tell which end of a worm is the front?

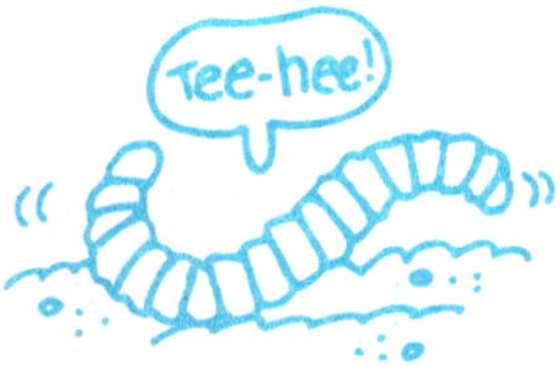

Two Stars for You!

Ending Consonant r

Print the answers to the riddles on the lines. Find the words in the starfish.

You ride in me.

I am a ____________________ .

I shine in the sky at night.

I am a ____________________ .

I have antlers. My baby is a fawn.

I am a ____________________ .

You open and close me.

I am a ____________________ .

What do you throw out when you want to use it, but take in when you don't want to use it?

Ollie Octopus

Ending Consonant s

Write the words that end with s in the treasure chest.

What did the girl octopus ask the boy octopus on their first date?

You're the Boss!

Ending Consonant s

Print the answers to the riddles on the lines. Find the words in the starfish.

You put me in your car.

I am ______________________ .

You can ride me to school.

I am a ______________________ .

I tell people what to do.

I am the ______________________ .

Girls can wear me.

I am a ______________________ .

What part of a fish weighs the most?

Say These Out Loud!

Ending Consonants f and s

Say the name of each picture. Print the letter sound you hear at the end of each word.

What kind of fish tastes best with bread and peanut butter?

Here's that Silly Sea Serpent!

Ending Consonant t

Find the words ending in t in the silly sea serpent. Print them on the lines.

Why did the frog cross the ocean on a surfboard?

A Cat in a Hat

Ending Consonant t

Say the name of each picture. Print the letters to complete each word. Color the pictures.

b ______

m ______

c ______

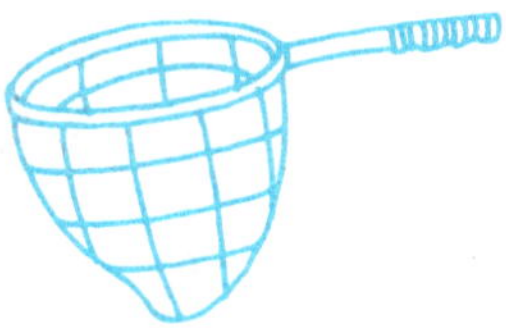

n ______

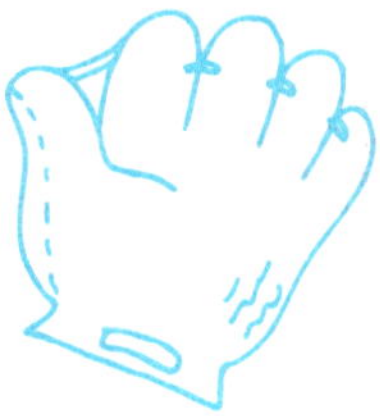

m ______

n ______

What is full of holes but holds water?

Fat Cat

Ending Consonant t

Look at the picture. Print the correct word to complete each sentence.

This is a ____________ .
(pat, cat)

He is ____________ .
(fat, mat)

He ____________ on the ____________ .
(sat, mat) (hat, pat)

Now the hat is ____________ .
(bat, flat)

What two-word rhyme describes a way to travel around a castle?

A Goat in a Boat

Ending Consonant t

Look at the picture. Print the correct word in each sentence.

I am a ____________________ .

(moat, goat)

I have on a ____________________ .

(coat, boat)

I am in a ____________________ .

(boat, throat)

It can ____________________ .

(float, coat)

When does a boat show affection?

Far Out!

Ending Consonants r and t

Say the name of each picture. Print the letter sound you hear at the end of each word.

Why is the river rich?

More Review!

Ending Consonants g, n, r, and t

Say the name of each picture. Print the letter sound you hear at the end of each word.

pi

su

goa

pea

lio

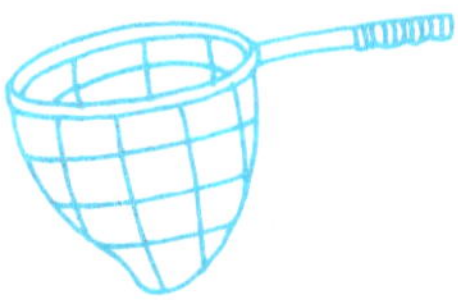

ne

What card game do cats like to play?

How Do These End?

Ending Consonants b, m, p, and t

Say the name of each picture. Write the letter sound you hear at the end of each word.

dru

an

we

mo

What do you get if you cross a boy scout with a shark?

"X" Marks the Spot

Ending Consonant x

Say the name of each picture. Draw a line from the large X to words that end with the sound of x.

What two-word rhyme describes the king frog's wife?

Silly Sea Serpent

Ending Consonant x

Find the words ending in x in the silly sea serpent. Print them on the lines.

If you throw a white stone into the Pacific Ocean on a dark night, what does it become?

Bob the Fox

Ending Consonants b and x

Circle the letter you hear at the end of each word.

x
p
g

d
x
t

g
n
b

b
t
n

g
t
x

How can you spell hard water with only three letters?

Lots of Ending Consonants!

Ending Consonants k, r, s, and x

Say the name of each picture. Write the letter sound you hear at the end of each word.

hoo

doo

bu

fo

How can you tell if there is a whale in your bathtub?

You Know These!

Review

Print the letter sound you hear at the end of each word.

What did they call the duck who fell in the soup?

You're Good at This!

Review

Print the ending letter for each picture.

ba

we

su

si

bo

ha

po

fa

te

Why are fish poor tennis players?

You've Got It Now!

Review

Circle the letter you hear at the end of each word.

What's the easiest way to catch a fish?